A Guide for Using

A Year Down Yonder

in the Classroom

Based on the book written by
Richard Peck

*This guide written by **Sarah Kartchner Clark, M.A.***

Teacher Created Resources, Inc.
6421 Industry Way
Westminster, CA 92683
www.teachercreated.com
ISBN: 978-0-7439-3156-4
©2002 Teacher Created Resources, Inc.
Reprinted, 2013
Made in U.S.A.

Edited by
Eric Migliaccio

Illustrated by
Wendy Chang

Cover Art by
Wendy Chang

Table of Contents

Introduction 3

Sample Lesson Plans 4

Before the Book (*Pre-reading Activities*) 5

About the Author 6

Book Summary 7

Vocabulary Lists 8

Vocabulary Activities 9

Section 1 ("Prologue" & "Rich Chicago Girl") 10
  - Quiz Time
  - Hands-on Project—Background Information
  - Cooperative Learning—Literature Discussion Group
  - Curriculum Connections—*Writing*: Writing an Essay
  - Into Your Life—Journal Jar

Section 2 ("Vittles and Vengeance") 15
  - Quiz Time
  - Hands-on Project—Apple Sculptures
  - Cooperative Learning—Debating the Issues
  - Curriculum Connections—*English*: Diagramming Sentences
  - Into Your Life—Letter to Grandma

Section 3 ("A Minute in the Morning" & "Away in a Manger") 20
  - Quiz Time
  - Hands-on Project—Simple Yet Substantial
  - Cooperative Learning—Round-Robin Questions
  - Curriculum Connections—*Social Studies*: Time Line of Events
  - Into Your Life—Poetry Passages

Section 4 ("Hearts and Flour") 25
  - Quiz Time
  - Hands-on Project—In the Dough!
  - Cooperative Learning—Themes and Things
  - Curriculum Connections—*Math*: Now and Then
  - Into Your Life—Character Comparisons

Section 5 ("A Dangerous Man," "Gone with the Wind," & "Ever After") . . . 30
  - Quiz Time
  - Hands-on Project—Developing a New Character
  - Cooperative Learning—Literary Elements
  - Curriculum Connections—*Science*: Tornadoes
  - Into Your Life—Newsy Notes

After the Book (*Post-reading Activities*)
  - Writing a Review 35
  - Book Report Ideas 36
  - Historical-Fiction Analysis 37
  - Culminating Activities 38
  - Unit Test Options 43

Bibliography of Related Sources 46

Answer Key 47

Introduction

Literature opens the door to magical new worlds. Historical fiction novels are an engaging genre of literature that is quick to read and yet leaves a lasting impression. Within the pages of a story are words, vocabulary, and characters that can inspire us to achieve our highest ideals. We can turn to stories for companionship, recreation, comfort, and guidance.

By engaging our imaginations and emotions, stories let us learn about people we may never meet and explore places to which we may never go. The best stories also help us discover more about ourselves. Like a good friend, a good story touches and enriches our lives forever.

In *Literature Units*, great care has been taken to select books that are sure to become good friends.

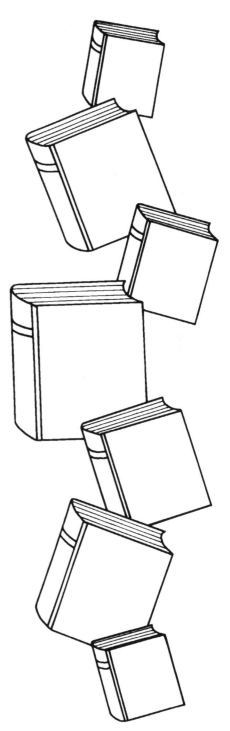

Teachers who use this literature unit will find the following features to supplement their own valuable ideas:

- Sample Lesson Plans
- Pre-reading Activities
- Biographical Sketch and Picture of Author
- Book Summary
- Vocabulary Lists and Suggested Vocabulary Activities
- Chapters grouped for study, with each section including:
    —quizzes
    —hands-on projects
    —cooperative learning activities
    —cross-curriculum connections
    —extensions into the reader's own life
- Post-reading Activities
- Research Ideas
- Book Report Ideas
- Culminating Activities
- Three Different Options for Unit Tests
- Bibliography of Related Sources
- Answer Key

Using this unit as part of your teaching strategies can help you show your students how reading can touch their lives in wondrous ways.

Sample Lesson Plans

Each of the lessons suggested below can take from one to several days to complete.

Lesson 1
- Introduce and complete some or all of the pre-reading activities. (page 5)
- Read "About the Author." (page 6)
- Introduce the vocabulary list for Section 1. (page 8)

Lesson 2
- Read Section 1. As you read, place the vocabulary words in the context of the story and discuss their meanings.
- Choose a vocabulary activity. (page 9)
- Follow the directions to make a map of the town where the story takes place. (page 11)
- Participate in a literature discussion group and complete activities. (page 12)
- Follow the directions on writing an essay. (page 13)
- Begin the Journal Jar activity. (page 14)
- Administer Section 1 quiz. (page 10)
- Introduce the vocabulary list for Section 2. (page 8)

Lesson 3
- Read Section 2. As you read, place the vocabulary words in the context of the story and discuss their meanings.
- Choose a vocabulary activity. (page 9)
- Follow the directions for making apple sculptures. (page 16)
- Do the exercises on debating tips and techniques. (page 17)
- Complete the assignment on diagramming sentences. (page 18)
- Learn the importance of family relationships and write a letter to Grandma. (page 19)
- Administer Section 2 quiz. (page 15)
- Introduce the vocabulary list for Section 3. (page 8)

Lesson 4
- Read Section 3. As you read, place the vocabulary words in the context of the story and discuss their meanings.
- Choose a vocabulary activity. (page 9)
- Cook up a recipe of burgoo stew and cherry tarts. (page 21)
- Work with a group on the round-robin question activity. (page 22)

- Determine the events for the years 1935–1940 in U.S. history. (page 23)
- Learn about different types of poetry and create your cinquain, haiku, and limerick. (page 24)
- Administer Section 3 quiz. (page 20)
- Introduce the vocabulary list for Section 4. (page 8)

Lesson 5
- Read Section 4. As you read, place the vocabulary words in the context of the story and discuss their meanings.
- Choose a vocabulary activity. (page 9)
- Make the play dough and guess the vocabulary words and story events. (page 26)
- Participate in group activities dealing with themes from the story. (page 27)
- Use the chart of prices to solve math problems. (page 28)
- Compare experiences in your life to that of a character in the book. (page 29)
- Administer the Section 4 quiz. (page 25)
- Introduce the vocabulary list for Section 5. (page 8)

Lesson 6
- Read Section 5. As you read, place the vocabulary words in the context of the story and discuss their meanings.
- Choose a vocabulary activity. (page 9)
- Create the new, life-size character. (page 31)
- Learn the literary elements of a novel. (page 32)
- Make your own tornado and learn tornado safety tips. (page 33)
- Write your own newsy notes. (page 34)
- Administer the Section 5 quiz. (page 30)

Lesson 7
- Assign the book review, book report and historical fiction analysis. (page 35–37)
- Begin work on culminating activities. (pages 38–42)

Lesson 8
- Administer Unit Tests 1, 2, and/or 3. (pages 43–45)
- Provide a list of related reading materials for your students. (page 46)

4

Before the Book

Before students begin reading *A Year Down Yonder*, have them participate in some pre-reading activities to stimulate interest and enhance their comprehension of this story.

1. Set up a book display of a variety of historical fiction books that were written during the Depression. There are numerous titles that are available and many that have been award-winning novels. See the bibliography (page 46) for suggestions. Allow students time to browse and read some of these stories. Ask students to write down observations they have gathered about stories written about the Depression.

2. As a class, discuss the characteristics of historical-fiction stories. How are historical fiction stories different than mysteries, romance novels, poetry, research reports, essays, etc.?

3. Show a picture of Richard Peck (page 6) and have some of his other stories on display for students to look at and read.

4. Read about Richard Peck (page 6). Review some aspects of his life with the students. Discuss the following questions:

   - Richard Peck used to teach school. How does being a teacher prepare you to become an author of books written for children?

   - Do you think being a high school teacher helps you understand the needs of young adults?

   - Who do you think is qualified to write about issues that teenagers struggle with?

   - Who are some of your favorite authors? Are you familiar with their backgrounds?

5. Distribute copies of *A Year Down Yonder*. Have students look at the cover and title. Spend some time as a class discussing the book. Be sure to have students share their predictions on what they think the story will be about. Have the students ever read other books by Richard Peck? If so, are there things about his style that will probably appear in this book as well?

6. Read aloud the prologue of the book. Have students draw illustrations of their interpretation of the story. Have students share their illustrations with their classmates and discuss other observations they have about *A Year Down Yonder* so far.

7. Discuss the following questions with students:

   - Are one or both of your grandmothers living?

   - What is your grandmother(s) like?

   - How well do you get along with your grandmother?

   - How would you feel about going to live with your grandmother?

   - What adjustments would you have to make if you went to live with your grandmother?

   - What are some neat things you know about your grandmother?

About the Author

Richard Peck was born on April 5, 1934, and he grew up in Decatur, Illinois. Peck dreamed of living in New York and going to London. He ended up getting to do both. Peck attended Exeter University in England, and later received degrees at DePaul University and Southern Illinois University. He is currently living in New York City.

Richard Peck has written over 20 novels and has won many awards. Some of the awards he has won include the 1990 Margaret A. Edwards Award, the 1990 National Council of Teachers of English/ALAN Award for outstanding contributions to young adult literature, the 1991 Medallion from the University of Southern Illinois, and the Mystery Writers of America Edgar Allan Poe Award. In 2001 Richard Peck won the Newbery Medal for *A Year Down Yonder*.

Peck credits his mother for being a strong influence on him as a writer: She read to him before he could read. He had teachers that influenced him as well. Richard Peck eventually became a teacher himself. He taught high school English but soon became discouraged, so he quit teaching and began writing. Writing books for young adults gives him a way to still work with young adults in mind. He continues to travel around the country meeting with young adults to get ideas for novels.

Richard Peck taught junior high, high school, and college English. He was also the Assistant Director of the Council for Basic Education in Washington, D.C. Other jobs Peck has held include being a ghostwriter of sermons for army chaplains and a textbook editor. Peck has also written and published poetry, and he currently writes about architecture for *The New York Times*.

Peck's books deal with issues that young adults are facing. He explores contemporary issues such as peer pressure, censorship, single parenting, suicide, death, and rape. He takes the plights of teens seriously, and his books are written with the intent to inform and to encourage. He claims that his books are inspired by observing and eavesdropping on the lives of young people.

His advice to young readers who wish to write is to learn new vocabulary words. Learning at least five new words a day can help young writers develop their skills. He also encourages the study of Latin, as it can help writers learn the system of how the English language is put together.

Other books written by Peck include *The Ghost Belonged to Me, Close Enough to Touch, Ghosts I Have Been, The Dreadful Future of Blossom Culp, Are You in the House Alone?, Remembering the Good Times, Those Summer Girls I Never Met, Unfinished Portrait of Jessica, Secrets of the Shopping Mall, Voices After Midnight*, and *Strays Like Us*. Some of these books have been made into television movies. Peck's *A Long Way From Chicago* is a series of seven short stories written by Peck. These stories are about the character Mary Alice and her brother Joey.

A Year Down Yonder

by Richard Peck

(Dial Books for Young Readers, 2000)
(Available in CAN, UK, and AUS from Penguin)

Mary Alice learns that she is to live with her Grandma Dowdel in a small town outside of Chicago. The story begins with Mary Alice on the train heading for Grandma's. Things wouldn't be so bad except that Grandma Dowdel isn't your typical Grandma. She's crazy—or so it seems at first. Mary Alice soon learns to get used to Grandma's crazy antics and learns to recognize the humor and love that Grandma has.

Mary Alice's year with Grandma turns out to be filled with adventures. From wrecking tractors, to sponsoring rip-roaring parties, Grandma is a piece of work. This year will not be a quiet one for Mary Alice.

Though Grandma is not affectionate, she has her own ways of showing love and care. The whole town seems to step aside when Grandma comes along. Mary Alice watches as Grandma stirs things up in town and settles things down at home. She sees Grandma distract Mildred Burdick out of bullying a dollar out of Mary Alice, trap foxes, curtail the intentions of youngsters set to tip over her privy, and send Maxine Patch racing through town without any clothes on.

Mary Alice learns a lot by living with Grandma. She learns to cook and roll out pie dough from the inside out. She also learns how a fox can be trapped; how to live with hardly any money; and how to make do with what you have and maybe with what others have, too!

Mary Alice learns more about who she is by living with Grandma. She learns to be independent of the crowd and to take care of herself. Grandma Dowdel subtly teaches Mary Alice to be thrifty and self-sufficient. The lessons Mary Alice learns the year she lived with Grandma stay with her and prompt her to return when she is older, marrying in Grandma Dowdel's home and beginning a new chapter of her life.

Though Mary Alice came to the hick town with remorse and regret, she walked away a better person. She could easily have seen Grandma as strange and crazy, but instead she saw a fun, outgoing woman with an imagination to come out on top in every situation. Just what you need to make it through your teenage years at the end of the Great Depression!

Vocabulary Lists

On this page are vocabulary lists that correspond to each section. Vocabulary activity ideas can be found on page 9 of this book.

Section 1

recession	woe	milled
conservation	kin	astride
privy	teetered	wary
trudged	threshold	clabber
conniption	celluloid	penitentiary
swaybacked	rasped	cadavers
cipher	trilled	

Section 2

vittles	berth	shucking
waging	adder	wan
piteous	haste	shied
doled	foliage	splayed
surged	transfixed	sullen
coroner	reeled	vengeance
coronary	heady	

Section 3

scuttled	pelting	jaunty
chink	headlong	swathed
sulky	utter	palsy
dungarees	brigade	slouch
milled	slack-mouthed	preened
forlorn		chancel
veered	jostled	

Section 4

scrapple	gaggle	lurched
capitulated	savor	bleakly
aristocracy	gaped	corduroy
benediction	pecking	argyle
citified	fumbled	grappled
rapping	hemline	flimsy
sniffy		

Section 5

aglow	mirth	lashing
scruff	dubious	venturing
scudding	prim	annihilating
per diem	presided	hazarded
audible	temperament	snit
wary	cruets	
annals	chaff	

8

Vocabulary Activities

Help your students learn and retain the necessary vocabulary for *A Year Down Yonder* by providing them with interesting vocabulary activities.

Five or Fewer

Instruct students to select five vocabulary words to use in a paragraph. To make it more challenging, have the students try to pick different parts of speech (e.g., nouns, verbs, and adjectives).

Characterization

Have each student select a character from the story. Then, have each student write a description of this character without using the character's name. Students must use vocabulary words in the descriptions. Students then share the descriptions aloud and see if classmates can figure out the characters being described.

Categorically Speaking

Have students categorize all of the vocabulary words into the different parts of speech—nouns, verbs, adjectives, etc. Students may use a dictionary to double check and see if words have been labeled correctly. After locating all of the verbs, have students write all the verb endings for each verb. Then they can check the spelling and endings in the dictionary.

"Alphables"

Have students create "alphables" by listing the words in alphabetical order and dividing them into syllables.

Race Against Time

Write the vocabulary words on index cards. Divide students into two teams. One person at a time draws a vocabulary word from the pile of index cards. Decide on a time limit. The student must then describe the word, without using any form of the word, to his/her team. If the word or a form of the word is used, no point is given. A point is given if the word is defined correctly. If time remains, the student can draw another word and try for another point. Play continues until time runs out. The team adds up and records its points. The opposing team then has a turn to compete for points.

It's All Write

Have students work in cooperative learning groups to write stories, using as many vocabulary words from the book as possible. Tell students to use the words in the same context that they were used in the book. Have students read their group stories aloud to the class.

High-Tech Vocabulary

Have students type vocabulary words onto the computer. They should then look up each word, using the thesaurus on the computer. Students then type in the meaning next to each vocabulary word.

Puzzling Predictions

Before looking up the definition of each word, have students write a prediction of what they think the word means. How close were they to the real definition?

Quiz Time

Answer the following questions about Section 1.

1. On the back of this paper, write a one-page summary of this section. Include a topic sentence that tells the main idea and at least three supporting details for the major events in each chapter.

2. What is the name of the main character? How old is she? _____

   _____

3. Who are the members of the main character's immediate family?_____

   _____

4. Why is Mary Alice going to live with her Grandma?_____

   _____

5. Where is the setting for the book?_____

   _____

6. Describe Grandma Dowdel._____

   _____

7. What two things did Mary Alice bring with her? Where is the first place Grandma took Mary Alice upon her arrival? _____

   _____

   _____

8. What is the high school like where Mary Alice will attend? _____

   _____

9. Why does Mary Alice owe Mildred Burdick a dollar? How does she get out of it?_____

   _____

   _____

10. Who is friendly with Mary Alice? Why are most of the girls not interested in her?

   _____

   _____

Background Information

A Year Down Yonder takes place in a fictional town outside of Chicago, Illinois, at the end of the Great Depression. What do you picture in your mind when you think of the setting to this story? Complete the following activities to establish the setting.

1. Based on the picture on the cover, what do you think the small town looks like? What is the climate? What types of plants and trees grow there? _____

    _____

    _____

    _____

2. Research small towns outside of Chicago. What are the weather patterns like? What plants and flora grow there? _____

    _____

    _____

3. Use maps to learn more about the location of the story. Is the terrain rugged or smooth? Are there mountains, oceans, or rivers in the surrounding area? _____

    _____

4. On a piece of construction paper, create a map of the town where *A Year Down Yonder* takes place. Location and places on the map will be determined by you. You are creating a fictional map. Maps will vary from one student to another. (This exercise is to help you visualize the setting of this story.) Be sure to include a compass and a key/legend. Start with a rough draft on a piece of paper. Determine what materials (markers, colored pencils, crayons, etc.) you will use to make your map.

5. Keep this map handy and add to it as you read this story. Whenever there is a new location or place mentioned in the story, add it to your map. Here are some places and locations to add to the map based on what you have read in the book so far:

    - train station
    - Grandma's house
    - the high school
    - the Coffee Pot Cafe

    - Moore's store
    - Weidenbach's bank
    - Old Man Nyquist's house

Parts of a Map

Directions—On the map, draw a compass rose with the direction words: north, south, east, and west.

Symbols—Symbols are miniature pictures drawn on a map. Symbols can include houses, trees, buildings, streets, bridges, and rivers.

Legend or Key—A key or legend explains the meaning of the symbols on the map. It is included to make it easier to understand the map.

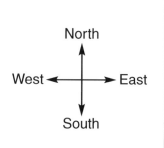

Literature Discussion Group

Literature discussion groups are a great way for you to share thoughts and ideas about what you are reading and a way to learn from each other. Working in discussion groups, you will discuss the "Prologue" and "Rich Chicago Girl" chapters from *A Year Down Yonder*. To prepare for your literature discussion, read these chapters and complete the questions on this page. Once you have completed this page, meet as a group to discuss your responses.

A. Write five questions that you can ask your group members about the pages you have just read. (Be sure that you can answer the questions you write!)

1. _____
    _____
2. _____
    _____
3. _____
    _____
4. _____
    _____
5. _____
    _____

B. Select an event from the story to discuss with your literature discussion group. On a separate piece of paper, write what you think happened. What is your opinion of what happened? Discuss this particular event as a group.

C. Select one of the following projects to bring and share with the literature discussion group:

  • Write a prediction about what you think will happen next in the story. Be sure to have evidence to back up your ideas.

  • Select five words from the story and write down many thoughts and words that are associated with these words. Discuss the definitions and the uses of these words from this story.

  • Select a character to portray. Dress up like the character and read a passage from the story about this character to your literature discussion group. Explain how you are alike or different than this character.

  • Write a one-week diary as though you were one of the characters from the story. Share your diary with your literature discussion group.

  • Draw a picture of an event from the story. See if your group can determine what event is being portrayed before you share the name of the event with them.

D. After meeting with your discussion group, answer the following questions on the back of this paper:

  • How well did you listen to the other members of the group?

  • How well were you able to answer the questions?

  • Did you participate in answering the questions of your group members?

  • How can you improve as a member or as a group in the literature discussion?

Writing an Essay

You are about to write an essay on the Great Depression, which took place during the 1930s. This is a fascinating time in history, and historians still debate and discuss the causes and effects of the Depression. Please use the following guidelines and suggestions below to help you write this essay.

Step 1: Selecting a Topic

There are many different topics that you could select to research and write about. Browse through books written on the topic and discuss possible topics with other students. Here are just a few topics to consider:

- Causes of the Great Depression
- Effects of the Great Depression
- Life in the 1930s
- Franklin and/or Eleanor Roosevelt
- The Stock Market
- The New Deal

Step 2: Outlining an Essay

Research Your Topic—Use a variety of materials like encyclopedias, books, the Internet, and interviews of people that lived during the Depression to research your topic. Be sure to write down notes to use for your rough draft.

Select the Main Idea—Your essay will need to have a thesis. (A thesis is the main point of an essay.) The author usually presents the thesis early in the essay and then uses evidence to prove the thesis. Here is a sample thesis statement: *The Great Depression began when the stock market crashed.* This essay would select three statements to support the evidence that the crash of the stock market caused the Depression.

Writing a Rough Draft—Don't worry about your rough draft being perfect. Use an outline to get all your ideas on paper. Select three or four main ideas that can support your thesis statement. Too many ideas can weaken the essay and make it unclear and difficult to read. Be sure you have enough research to support each main idea. Keep your rough draft as neat as possible.

Writing a Final Copy—Once you have researched and written the rough draft of your essay, you are ready to write the final version. If you have not typed your report, you should do so at this point. If you are using a computer, be sure to use the grammar check and spell check. The computer thesaurus can also be helpful when you are trying to find the right word. Even though you have checked your work on the computer, you must always read through and look for more changes. Remember to check for punctuation and format errors as well.

Step 3: Looking it Over

Other questions to ask after you have written your essay include the following:

- ❑ Does my essay have a title?
- ❑ Does my essay have a thesis?
- ❑ Is the thesis stated clearly at the beginning?
- ❑ Are there supportive paragraphs that support my thesis?
- ❑ Have I remembered the audience for whom I am writing?
- ❑ Have I concluded the essay appropriately?
- ❑ Have I made my point?
- ❑ Is my essay easy to read and follow?

Journal Jar

Throughout this unit, students will be asked to write down their thoughts, ideas, guesses, feelings, opinions, and suggestions. Getting students to write down these ideas is crucial to helping them make the connections in their lives to the history they are studying.

Directions: Use a glass jar (or other container) to hold the questions that students will write about in their journal. Cut out the strips of journal questions below and place them in the journal jar. Each student will need a notebook to use as a journal. Journal entries should be written and answered as honestly and as thoughtfully as possible. Be sure to have students write the date at the beginning of each journal entry. Each student's opinion might change from the beginning of the unit to the end. More information learned on a certain subject allows us to go into more depth and use critical thinking skills to solve problems and issues.

Here are a few questions that can be used in the journal jar. Cut these up and place them in the jar. As the unit progresses and the students have read more of the book, more questions can be added to the jar. Encourage students to add to the journal jar. Pull only one question from the jar each day.

1. What are your thoughts about those who are less fortunate? How can we help?

2. Why do you think Mildred Burdick is the way she is (mean, a bully, insecure, etc.)?

3. Name some adjectives to describe Grandma Dowdel. Is she a good or bad person? Explain.

4. What do you think about the way Grandma got pecans for her pie? How would you have felt if you were going with her?

5. Do you think Augie Fluke learned his lesson from Grandma Dowdel? What's your opinion of the incident?

6. How are young people today different than they were in the late 1930s and early 1940s?

7. Mary Alice lists Fibber McGee and Molly, Baby Snooks, and Edgar Bergen as some of the singers heard on the radio. Who are some of the singers heard on the radio today? How has music changed since the 1930s?

8. What was Armistice Day? Do we still celebrate Armistice Day? What is patriotism like in the United States today?

9. Do you think Grandma Dowdel invited Aunt Mae Griswold to the party to get the truth out about Mrs. Weidenbach?

10. Why do you think Grandma isn't a member of an organized group, such as the auxiliary or the DAR? Are you a member of a group? What do you gain by being a member of a group?

Extension: Create a parent/student journal. These same questions could be asked of the parents or grandparents of students in your class. Students will learn much from hearing the opinions and ideas of those that either lived through the Great Depression or had family experiences associated with it. What an opportunity to share, in an informal setting, feelings, emotions, and ideas across the generations!

Quiz Time

Answer the following questions about Section 2.

1. On the back of this paper, write a one-page summary of this section. Include a topic sentence that tells the main idea and at least three supporting details for the major events in each chapter.

2. What was Grandma planning on bringing to the Halloween party for refreshments? _____

    _____

3. Why does Grandma decide not to make gooseberry pies? _____

    _____

4. How did Grandma and Mary Alice get the pecans and the pumpkins for the pies?_____

    _____

    _____

5. How does Grandma justify taking the pumpkins? _____

    _____

6. What did Grandma prepare to ward off the pranksters who tried to knock over her privy? What happened when the pranksters came? _____

    _____

    _____

7. What did Augie Fluke look like at the Halloween party?_____

    _____

8. How do the townspeople feel about Grandma Dowdel?_____

    _____

9. What was the response of the townspeople about Grandma's pies?_____

    _____

10. How did Bootsie fall prey to the pranksters near Halloween? _____

    _____

Apple Sculptures

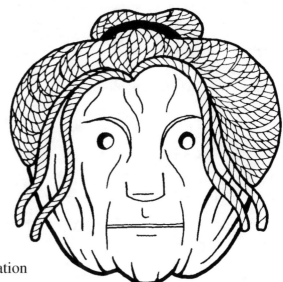

Materials

- a firm apple (not too ripe)
- a paring knife (not too sharp)
- cotton (cotton balls work fine)
- lemon juice
- bowl
- salt
- cookie sheet
- shellac
- cloves or pins for eyes, rice for teeth, etc.
- scraps of fabric, yarn, or other materials for decoration

Directions

1. First, determine which character from *A Year Down Yonder* that you would like to portray in your apple sculpture. Draw a sketch of what you think the character looks like. Use this sketch as you create your apple sculpture.

2. Peel the apple, taking off the skin but leaving as much of the apple in place as possible. Cut out the core of the apple and stuff the center with cotton.

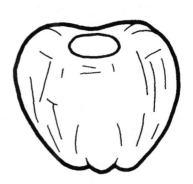

3. Carve features into the apple (eyes, mouth, and nose), but don't carve very deeply because the areas that are carved will seem even deeper once the apple has dried.

4. Pour lemon juice into a bowl. Dip the carved apple into the lemon juice. Then cover the apple with salt. This will keep your apple from shrinking too much. Place the apple on the cookie sheet. Write your name on a slip of paper so that your apple won't be confused with another student's apple.

5. Let the apple dry in a warm place for about four weeks; or, with adult assistance, you can dry it in an oven at 100°F (45°C) for five hours and then at room temperature for one week.

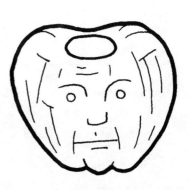

6. After the drying process, wash and dry the apple.

7. Cover the apple with shellac and let dry again. Add any fabric, yarn, or materials for decoration as desired. This apple sculpture can be used as a puppet head.

Debating the Issues

Whenever you look at an issue, there are always at least two sides to it. You will be asked to debate an issue that is found in *A Year Down Yonder*. Anticipating the questions the opposing view has makes for a more solid argument on your part. Eliminating questions that the opposition has is an effective tool when persuading people about a particular topic. Read each of the thesis statements below. Then write down opposing views that someone could have after reading these issues.

1. School uniforms should be mandatory.
2. Cassette tapes and CDs should have warning labels on them.
3. Every student should take summer school.
4. Halloween jokes and pranks should be tolerated and enjoyed.

Now select an issue to debate from *A Year Down Yonder*. Write down your opinion and supportive statements below. Then write down what someone of the opposing view might think. When planning your debate techniques, be sure to address these opposing views.

Your Opinion/Supportive Statements

_____

_____

_____

_____

Opposing View of the Issue/Supportive Statements

_____

_____

_____

_____

Debate Techniques and Tips

❑ Select and limit the subject you will be debating.

❑ Determine the overall purpose. What are you trying to persuade others to think?

❑ Analyze the audience and who you will be debating. Anticipate the opposition's arguments and assumptions.

❑ Organize your arguments. Divide them into the three parts of the presentation (opening, body, and conclusion).

❑ Practice your debate speech before you deliver it (several times, if possible).

Diagramming Sentences

In *A Year Down Yonder*, we read about how the students in Mary Alice's class were asked to diagram sentences. Complete the following exercises and see if this student work from the 1930s and 1940s resembles any work you are asked to do today.

Diagramming is a way to show relationships between parts. To diagram a sentence is to show the structure of a sentence and how all the parts fit together. This can help a writer determine grammatical errors in a sentence.

Here is a diagram for a simple sentence:

We	will race.
subject	verb

Diagram the following simple sentences. The first one has been done for you.

1. I am writing.

I	am writing.

2. I will respond.

3. She skis.

4. Andy swims.

Here is the diagram for a simple sentence with adjectives or adverbs:

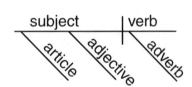

Diagram the following sentences. The first has been done for you.

5. The tall building burned quickly.

6. A big dog jumped happily.

7. The funny baby clapped joyfully.

8. Two angry men yelled loudly.

9. The new teacher spoke well.

Extension: On the back of this paper, write a simple sentence. Exchange your sentence with another student and have him or her diagram your sentence. Was it done correctly?

Letter to Grandma

The story begins with Mary Alice being a bit afraid of Grandma Dowdel and the prospect of living with her. As the story progresses, these fears subside. Mary Alice learns more and more about her grandmother. What is your relationship with your grandma like? When was the last time you wrote a letter to your grandma? How much do you know about your grandma? Answer the following questions:

Special Note: If you do not have a grandmother that is still living, complete this activity about your grandfather or another senior citizen who is close to you.

Questions to Consider

1. Where was your grandmother born?

2. What was her family background like?

3. Did your grandma live during the Depression? What was life like for her as a child?

4. What do you like best about your grandma?

5. What lessons have you learned from your grandma?

6. How does your grandma feel about you? How do you know?

7. What can you do to improve the relationship with your grandma?

8. What do you think your grandma thinks about young people today?

9. Why is it sometimes difficult to relate to people from another generation?

10. How does Mary Alice feel about her grandma? What changes take place in the story in the relationship between Mary Alice and her grandma?

Writing a Letter

Using the information from the questions above, write a letter (or an e-mail message) to your grandma. Ask her questions and express how you feel about your relationship so that you are more likely to get a response.

A friendly letter has the date, a salutation (greeting), the body of the letter, a closing, and a signature. Don't forget to keep it neat and easy to read. Write the rough draft or outline version on the back of this paper.

You may choose to design your own stationery on the computer or use some personal stationery from home. Don't forget to follow through and mail the letter!

Quiz Time

Answer the following questions about Section 3.

1. On the back of this paper, write a one-page summary of this section. Include a topic sentence that tells the main idea and at least three supporting details for the major events in each chapter.

2. What did Grandma say when Mary Alice complained about the cold? _____

   _____

3. What is a turkey shoot? _____

   _____

4. What did Grandma say to the invitation to join the Auxiliary? _____

   _____

5. How did Grandma earn so much money for the burgoo? _____

   _____

6. What happened to poor Augie Fluke at the turkey shoot? _____

   _____

7. What happened to Mrs. Abernathy's son in the Great War? (Note: The Great War eventually became known as World War I.) _____

   _____

8. For what did Grandma trudge out in the snow in the middle of the night? _____

   _____

   _____

9. How was Carleen upstaged at the Christmas program? Whose baby was it? _____

   _____

   _____

   _____

10. Who was the invited guest who came to the Christmas program with Grandma? Where did Grandma get the money for the ticket? _____

   _____

Simple Yet Substantial

Food was as scarce as money during the Great Depression. Folks found recipes that called for simple ingredients. Burgoo was a common soup made during the Depression. It consists of meat and vegetables that are cooked for several hours until the flavors have blended and the ingredients have become a thick stew. Burgoo was originally cooked in iron kettles over a wood-burning fire, which gave the soup a smoky flavor. The name *burgoo* may come from the word *bulghur*, which is a form of cracked wheat, or *ragout* (pronounced *ragoo*), a French word for a well-seasoned stew. There are many different recipes available. Try this recipe—don't be afraid to add some ingredients of your own.

Burgoo

Ingredients

- 1 pound (.4 kg) of cooked meat (beef, lamb, pork, chicken, etc.)
- ½ gallon (2 L) chicken stock
- ½ gallon (2 L) beef stock
- 1 ounce Worcestershire sauce
- 1 cup (240 mL) tomatoes, diced
- 1 large onion, diced
- 1 celery stalk, diced

- 1 small green pepper, diced
- 1 large potato, diced
- 2 large carrots, diced
- ¼ cup (60 mL) peas
- ½ cup (120 mL) corn
- 2 teaspoons (10 mL) garlic, minced
- salt and pepper to taste

Directions: Combine all the ingredients and bring to a boil. Reduce heat and simmer for two hours, skimming the top as needed.

Cherry Tarts

Grandma Dowdel was known for her delicious cherry tarts. Try this delicious recipe and see whether these tarts would be fit for the Daughters of the American Revolution. This recipe serves eight.

Ingredients (serves 8)
- 6 tablespoons (90 mL) butter, cut into small pieces
- 1½ cups (360 mL) plus 2 tablespoons (30 mL) all-purpose flour
- 4 tablespoons (60 mL) cold water
- 3 tablespoons (45 mL) sugar
- 2 pounds (.9 kg) fresh cherries, pitted

Directions

1. With a fork or pastry blender, combine 1½ cups of the flour and the butter. Mix until the mixture forms a ball.

2. Using a rolling pin, roll out the dough into a circle about 13" (32.5 cm) in diameter and about ¼" (.6 cm) in thickness. (Remember to roll from the center out, as Grandma Dowdel suggests!)

3. Pick up the dough and place it over a 10½" (26.8 cm) tart pan. (A pie pan can be substituted.) Press the dough gently into the pan and refrigerate for 15 minutes. Preheat the oven to 375° F (190° C).

4. Blend the 2 tablespoons of flour with 1 tablespoon of the sugar. Sprinkle the bottom of the tart shell evenly with the flour mixture. Place the pitted cherries into the shell. Sprinkle the cherries with the remaining sugar and bake on the bottom rack of the oven for 45 minutes.

Extension: For extra practice with fractions, double the recipes on paper and try "halving" them.

Round-Robin Questions

Materials

- envelopes for each group of students
- copy of *A Year Down Yonder* for each student
- paper for each group of students

Directions

1. Divide students into groups of four or five. Assign the chapter and/or page numbers for the groups to read. Each group will be reading the same chapters and pages. Give each group an envelope. Have each group of students write their names on the front of the envelope.

2. Allow time for each group to read the assigned pages orally, with students taking turns reading passages and paragraphs. At the end of the reading, have members of each group write questions that could be asked and answered relating to the reading material just read. Each group needs to come up with five questions. Each of the five questions need to be formatted in one of the following ways:

   - true or false
   - fill in the blank
   - short essay
   - match the character (i.e., match the descriptions with the appropriate characters)
   - multiple choice

3. Once the questions have been written, students place the questions in the envelope provided. Now, have each group exchange their envelope with that of another group.

4. Each group answers the questions in the envelope submitted by a different group. (Each group writes the answers on a separate piece of paper—not on the same paper as the questions.) Groups must work together to come up with the answers. This is a cooperative group effort. Have one student serve as the scribe to write the answer to each question. Members of the group should refer to the book to find the answer. They should also be sure that each answer is complete and accurate before writing it down. Remind students that neatness counts!

5. Once students have finished answering the questions in the envelopes, the groups continue to exchange envelopes until all the groups have answered the questions submitted by each group in the class. Upon completion of this, groups return the envelopes to the groups of students whose names are written on the front.

6. When students receive their envelopes back, they read and grade each of the questions answered by the other groups. Were the questions answered correctly? They should refer groups to page numbers where they can locate the correct answer. Return the questions/papers back to the correct groups so they can see how they did.

7. Allow time for students to look over the answers they completed and turned in. Ask students what it was like to work in groups to answer comprehension questions. Is it easier to work independently? Why or why not?

Time Line of Events

Materials

- index cards
- colored pencils and markers
- reference materials (Internet, encyclopedias, books, etc.)
- yarn
- 6 pieces of 8½" x 11" paper

Directions

1. Write the years **1935**, **1936**, **1937**, **1938**, **1939**, and **1940** on each of six pieces of paper. These will be the year headings.

2. Attach to the wall a long piece of yarn around the perimeter of the classroom. Starting with 1935, attach the year headings along the yarn to form a time line. Be sure to space the year headings out to allow room for all the events.

3. Divide students into groups of four or five students. Assign each group one of the six years to research. They will be gathering information on what was going on during these years. Give each group a handful of index cards. Students will write the key events and dates that took place during their assigned year. Have students draw a small picture on the index card to illustrate each event. The index cards will be placed in the correct place on the time line.

Instructions for Students

After being divided into groups, you will be assigned a different year to research. The years that are being highlighted are 1935–1940. These are the years just before, during, and after the story takes place. This activity will give you a good picture of what was taking place during this time period.

Each group will research information and find events that took place during one of these years. Once your group has been assigned a year, you can use the Internet, encyclopedias, books, and individuals who lived during this time period to gather information. You will be putting key events, dates, and pictures on index cards that will be placed on the class time line.

Use the following topics as you begin your research:

- Famous People
- Inventions
- Entertainment
- Family Life
- Transportation
- Technology/Communication
- Education
- Clothing
- Food
- Government/Politics

Conclusion

Once all the dates and events have been placed on the time line, allow time for each group to give a brief presentation on the happenings during their year. Discuss as a class the differences between that time in U.S. history and now. How are things different? How are they the same? Did doing this activity help students understand the events and happenings in the story?

Poetry Passages

Poetry can bring ideas and images to life! Before writing a poem, you need to select a good subject or idea. For these poems, you will be using the characters from *A Year Down Yonder*. Consider the following characters from the story: Mary Alice, Grandma Dowdel, Joey, Mildred, Ina-Rae, Miss Butler, Augie Fluke, Old Man Nyquist, Carleen Lovejoy, Principal Fluke, Mrs. Abernathy, Mr. Herkimer, and Reverend Lutz. Each character will bring a different feeling to the poem. Brainstorm a list of descriptive words for each character. Select a character to use as the subject for your poem. You will be writing a word cinquain, a haiku, and a limerick. (Each poem needs to be about a different character from the book.)

Word Cinquain

A word cinquain is a poem that is five lines in length. Each line must contain a certain number of words.

  Line 1: Name of Character (1 word)
  Line 2: Description of Character (2 words)
  Line 3: Action about the Character (3 words)
  Line 4: Feeling about the Character (4 words)
  Line 5: Synonym for Description of Character in Line 2 (1 word)

Haiku

A haiku is a type of Japanese poetry that presents a picture of nature. The haiku you will write will represent a picture of a character. Haiku has three lines. The first line has five syllables, the second line has seven, and the third line has five.

  Brave at beginning,
  But caught in wire and glue.
  Augie needs more hair.

Limerick

A limerick is a humorous poem that has five lines. There is rhythm to a limerick. The first, second, and fifth lines rhyme. Lines three and four rhyme with each other. Lines one, two, and five have three stressed syllables; lines three and four have two.

  There once was a boy named Royce,
  who had a very quiet voice.
  He didn't give a hoot
  that they thought he was cute.
  He just never saw the need to make a choice!

Extension: Have a poetry reading as a class to share your poems with each other. A poetry reading demands a quiet and attentive audience that claps at the end of each reading.

Quiz Time

Answer the following questions about Section 4.

1. On the back of this paper, write a one-page summary of this section. Include a topic sentence that tells the main idea and at least three supporting details for the major events in each chapter.

2. Who is writing the "newsy notes"? _____

3. What is the DAR? What is the DAR organization asking Grandma Dowdel to make?

    _____

    _____

4. Who is Royce McNabb? Where does he come from? What does Carleen Lovejoy think about him? _____

    _____

5. Who sent Ina-Rae the valentines? How did Carleen Lovejoy respond? _____

    _____

6. What shocking news came out of the DAR party? _____

    _____

7. What is the ingredient that was added to Grandma's punch? _____

8. What do you think Grandma's intentions were of having the DAR party at her house?

    _____

    _____

9. What message did the pink, silk pillow have on it? Why do you think Grandma set it out when company came over? _____

    _____

10. Write your own question, based on the reading, and then answer it.

    _____

    _____

    _____

    _____

    _____

    _____

In the Dough!

Materials

- index card
- play dough (see recipe below)
- marker or pen
- timer

Directions

1. Make the recipe for play dough to use for this activity. You will need to make enough play dough for five or six groups of students. (This game will be played like the game Pictionary™, except with dough.)

2. Give each student five index cards. Have students write down or describe a scene, a character, or vocabulary words that can be found from the reading of *A Year Down Yonder*.

3. Divide your class into groups of four (or five, if needed.) Two people in each group will form a team. There will be two teams per group. Give each group a stack of index cards.

4. Select which team will go first in each group. The team that goes first will be using the dough to create the scene, describe the character, or describe the vocabulary word that is on the index card. Player A looks at the index card and uses the dough to communicate what is on the card. Player B tries to guess what is on the index card.

5. The other two members on the opposing team keep track of the time. Teams have two minutes (or some other predetermined amount of time established by group members) to guess the item on the index card.

6. If the first team is able to guess the item on the index card in the time allotted, then they receive a point and it is the next team's turn. Play continues until a team scores 10 points or the index cards are used up.

Play Dough Recipe

Ingredients

- 2 cups (480 mL) flour
- 1 cup (240 mL) salt
- 1 teaspoon (5 mL) cream of tartar
- 2 tablespoons (30 mL) oil
- 1 teaspoon (5 mL) food coloring
- 2 cups (480 mL) water

Directions: Mix ingredients in a saucepan. Cook over medium heat, stirring constantly until dough leaves sides of pan. Remove from pan, and cool until it can be touched. Knead for a few minutes.

Themes and Things

There are many themes in the book *A Year Down Yonder*. Here is a list of some of those themes that have been brought up in the book so far:

◆ Sacrifice   ◆ Being the New Kid

◆ Friendship   ◆ Endurance

◆ Family Relationships   ◆ Humor

◆ Hope   ◆ Survival

Can you add any more themes to this list? Select one of the themes from this book and design a project that represents this theme.

Project Ideas

- Write a skit about the theme you selected. Work together to create the setting, the characters, the plot, the climax, and the ending. You may choose to use some of the characters from the book as well as new ones in your skit.

- Interview family members or neighbors that lived through the Depression. Ask them about skills that they used to make it through those tough times. Have each member of your group conduct an interview. Compare and analyze the information you gather. What is a common theme you find?

- Watch a video that takes place during the Depression. (See the bibliography on page 46 for suggestions.) Take notes on the different themes that stand out as you watch the video. Compare the lives of those in the movie with that of Mary Alice. How are they similar or different?

- Write a group story about being the new kid on the block. Determine the main character and story line. Assign each group member a chapter of the book to write. Work together to blend the chapters together. Be sure to edit and review the story before you turn it in.

- Select a portion from the chapter entitled "Hearts and Flour" that your group finds humorous. Write a stand-up comedy script based on this event. Decide how each member of the group will participate and perform this stand-up comedy to the class. Prepare props and costumes that might be needed.

- Select somebody in your school to whom your group could give some attention. Write notes of encouragement. Perhaps there is someone who is ill, just lost a family member, or whose parents are getting divorced. Think of another act of kindness your group could do to spread hope.

- As a group, make a list of 10 or more people that you think represent the word *endurance*. Determine as a group, what the criteria is for someone to be placed on this list. Lead a class discussion. What do these people have in common? What characteristics do they have for enduring?

- As a group, cut out pictures from magazines and newspapers that represent friendship. Make a collage of all of these pictures. Have each group member share the name of a friend they appreciate. Then have each group member write a thank you note to that friend.

- Discuss as a group how important family relationships are. Then create video cards that group members can send to family members who live far away. Take turns videotaping each other. Discuss the importance of keeping these relationships alive.

Now and Then

How much have prices increased since the Great Depression? The chart below shows the price of food in American cities during 1933. Use a local grocery store advertisement or take a trip to the grocery store to find the prices for these items today. Complete the activities below to compare the prices.

Retail Food Prices					
Item	**Unit**	**1930s Prices**	**Prices Today**	**Difference**	**Percentage of Increase**
pork chops	pound	$0.20			
chuck roast	pound	$0.16			
bacon	pound	$0.23			
milk (delivered)	quart	$0.10			
eggs	dozen	$0.29			
butter	pound	$0.28			
flour	five pounds	$0.20			
bread	pound loaf	$0.07			

Activities

1. Find the difference between the price of each item in 1933 and its price today. Record your answers in the Difference column on the chart.

2. Look at the Difference column. Which items have increased the most? What has increased the least? Why do you think this is so?

3. What items can you purchase in a store today that you would not have been able to purchase during the Depression?

4. People today make more money than they did in 1933. The first federal minimum wage was set at $0.25 per hour. How much did a person make if he or she worked 40 hours a week at that minimum wage?

5. Find out what the federal minimum wage is today. How much would a worker earn today for 40 hours at the current minimum wage?

6. How much have prices increased since 1933? One way to analyze the data in the chart is to find the percent of increase for each item. Use this formula to calculate the percent of increase:

[(price today—1933 price) ÷ 1933 price] 100 = percent of increase

Character Comparisons

Compare yourself with a character from *A Year Down Yonder*. Write one or more words in each box. Use the headings as a guide. Answer the questions at the bottom of the page.

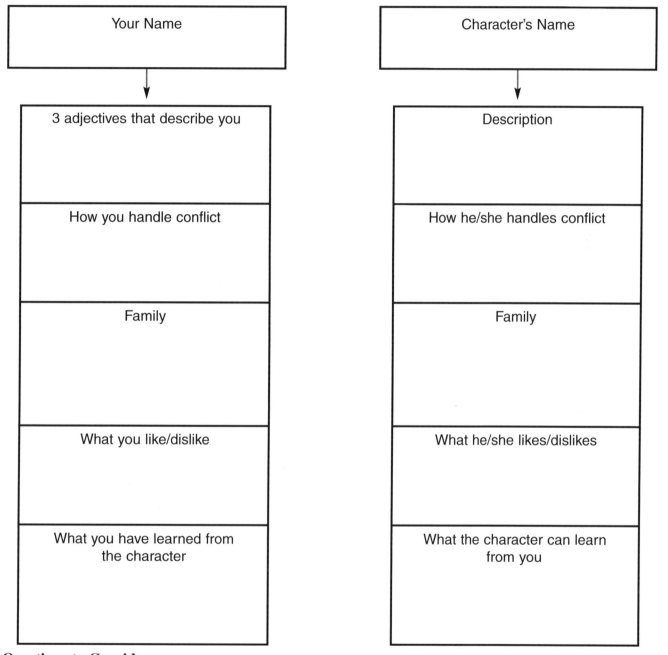

Your Name	Character's Name
3 adjectives that describe you	Description
How you handle conflict	How he/she handles conflict
Family	Family
What you like/dislike	What he/she likes/dislikes
What you have learned from the character	What the character can learn from you

Questions to Consider

1. Some characters remain in our memory for a long time. Will this character be a part of you?

2. Will Mary Alice or other characters from this book remain with you?

3. What in the character you compared yourself to makes him or her likeable?

4. What types of characters do you like in a book?

5. Who is your favorite character in this book so far?

Quiz Time

Answer the following questions about Section 5.

1. On the back of this paper, write a one-page summary of this section. Include a topic sentence that tells the main idea and at least three supporting details for the major events in each chapter.

2. What surprise in April did Bootsie leave on Mary Alice's bed?_____

3. Who did Mary Alice invite over to tutor her in math? _____

4. What does the tutor say that Mary Alice and he have in common? _____

5. What event happened while Mary Alice was being tutored? _____

   _____

6. How did Grandma alert the town about Maxine Patch? _____

   _____

7. How did the town respond to the incident?_____

   _____

8. Why did Grandma think Mary Alice should invite her teacher, Miss Butler, to dinner?

   _____

   _____

9. Why did Mary Alice race home in the middle of a tornado? Who was the first person Grandma went to check on after the tornado? _____

   _____

10. What is the relationship between Mary Alice and Grandma like? How does the story end? Did it end how you expected? _____

    _____

    _____

    _____

    _____

    _____

Developing a New Character

You have just been issued the challenge of creating a new character for *A Year Down Yonder*. The character needs to be credible and necessary.

Step 1

Answer the questions below to create a new story character of your own.

Character's Name: _____

Character's Description (age, looks, demeanor): _____

_____

_____

Character's Goal (What things are in the way of your character accomplishing this goal?):

_____

_____

_____

Character's Likes and Dislikes: _____

_____

_____

Character's Strengths and Fears: _____

_____

_____

What the character says and does: _____

_____

_____

Will this character be a friend or foe to Mary Alice? _____

_____

How well do Mary Alice and Grandma know this character? _____

_____

Step 2

Using a large piece of paper, trace a figure of this character. (You may trace the body of another classmate.) Color this body-sized figure and add accessorie—such as a scarf, necklace, or sunglasses—if desired.

Step 3

Write a chapter to introduce this new character into the plot. You may select where in the story you would like this character to appear.

Step 4

Share your new character and read the chapter to your class. Have a contest to determine which of the characters are most credible and necessary.

Literary Elements

To understand literature, it is important to understand the elements that can be found in literary passages. Working in groups of three or four, determine and locate the story elements that can be found in *A Year Down Yonder*. Discuss each of the elements listed below. Have one member of your group be the scribe to record group responses. When finished, compare your answers with those of the other groups.

Plot
(overall plan for the story)

Theme
(the main idea the writer wishes to convey)

Characterization
(the way a writer makes the reader aware of the characteristics
and motives of the characters in the story)

Style
(the writer's way of expressing thought—choice of words and manner of expression)

Setting
(the time and place in which the story takes place)

Tornadoes

While staying with her grandma, Mary Alice experiences a tornado. Just what is a tornado? A tornado is a powerful, twisting windstorm. The winds in a tornado are the most violent winds that can naturally occur on Earth. These winds can reach as fast as 200 miles per hour. A tornado is like a rotating funnel. Not all funnels reach the ground, while other funnels will dip down and touch the ground more than once. It is easy to create a homemade tornado of your own. Try these two recipes.

Method 1

Materials

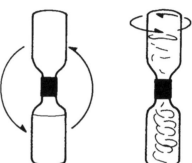

- 2 two-liter plastic bottles
- water

Directions

Take two 2-liter plastic bottles and fill one of them with water. Using duct tape, tape the empty soda bottle upside down on top of the bottle filled with water. Turn the bottle with water over and give the bottles a twist. A rotating circulation of water will flow into the bottle without water.

Method 2

Materials

- mayonnaise or canning jar with lid
- food coloring
- liquid dishwashing detergent
- vinegar

Directions

1. Fill a mayonnaise jar about ¾ full of water.
2. Add food coloring to the water, along with a teaspoon of liquid detergent and a teaspoon of vinegar.
3. Tighten the lid on the jar. Shake the jar vigorously, then give it a twist. The liquid will form a vortex (a rotating circulation) that looks like a small tornado. It will get longer and then shorten just like a real tornado.

Tornado Safety Tips

- Just like in the book, a basement, storm cellar, or the lowest place in a building is where you should be during a tornado.
- If you do not have a basement, you should go to an inner hallway or a room without windows.
- Stay away from any windows. Go to the center of the room.
- Get under a piece of sturdy furniture, such as a heavy table or desk, and hold onto it.
- Never try to drive ahead of a tornado in a car or truck. Tornadoes change directions quickly, and it is easy to get caught in a tornado and be thrown into the air. Get out of the car or truck immediately and take shelter in a nearby building or in a ditch or low area if there is not a building.

Newsy Notes

The "Newsy Notes From Our Communities" found in the local newspaper were written by Mary Alice. Look at the headlines below and write the "notes" that could go along with each headline.

GIRL 'NABS' NEW BOY AS TUTOR

_____

_____

SNAKE STARTLES ARTIST, TUTOR, STUDENT, AND TOWN!

_____

_____

TORNADO RIPS THROUGH TOWN AND HOME

_____

_____

Now write the headlines and notes of things that are going on in your life. What "newsy notes" could be written about events in your home, your school, or your community? Share your "newsy notes" with the class.

Headline: _____

_____

_____

_____

Headline: _____

_____

_____

_____

> **Extension:** Using the "newsy notes" written by members of your class, create a class newspaper, or post the notes on the school Web site. Select a member of your class to be the editor to help coordinate and organize all of the "newsy notes."

Writing a Review

Writing a review of a book, movie, or play takes preparation. Writing a review is more than stating your opinion. In order to have a balanced review, you must take into consideration the viewpoint of others that might read the book or watch the play. Look at the sample below of a movie review.

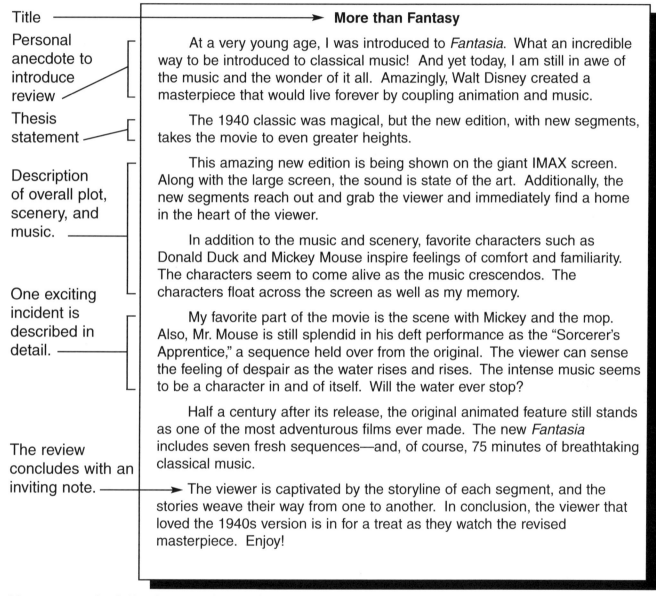

Title ————→ **More than Fantasy**

Personal anecdote to introduce review

At a very young age, I was introduced to *Fantasia*. What an incredible way to be introduced to classical music! And yet today, I am still in awe of the music and the wonder of it all. Amazingly, Walt Disney created a masterpiece that would live forever by coupling animation and music.

Thesis statement

The 1940 classic was magical, but the new edition, with new segments, takes the movie to even greater heights.

Description of overall plot, scenery, and music.

This amazing new edition is being shown on the giant IMAX screen. Along with the large screen, the sound is state of the art. Additionally, the new segments reach out and grab the viewer and immediately find a home in the heart of the viewer.

In addition to the music and scenery, favorite characters such as Donald Duck and Mickey Mouse inspire feelings of comfort and familiarity. The characters seem to come alive as the music crescendos. The characters float across the screen as well as my memory.

One exciting incident is described in detail.

My favorite part of the movie is the scene with Mickey and the mop. Also, Mr. Mouse is still splendid in his deft performance as the "Sorcerer's Apprentice," a sequence held over from the original. The viewer can sense the feeling of despair as the water rises and rises. The intense music seems to be a character in and of itself. Will the water ever stop?

Half a century after its release, the original animated feature still stands as one of the most adventurous films ever made. The new *Fantasia* includes seven fresh sequences—and, of course, 75 minutes of breathtaking classical music.

The review concludes with an inviting note.

The viewer is captivated by the storyline of each segment, and the stories weave their way from one to another. In conclusion, the viewer that loved the 1940s version is in for a treat as they watch the revised masterpiece. Enjoy!

Now answer the following questions to help you write a book review of *A Year Down Yonder*.

- What is your opinion of the book? Why do you think this?
- What might someone else (such as your parent, teacher, or friend) think about the book?
- What might someone with an opposing opinion say about your opinion of the book? Have you considered the alternative opinion?
- Who is your intended audience for this book review? Write accordingly.
- Write the thesis statement for your book review.
- List at least three examples from the book to support your opinion and statement.
- How will you conclude your review?

Book Report Ideas

There are numerous ways to report on a book. After you have finished *A Year Down Yonder*, choose one of the book report ideas to complete. Be prepared to share your book report with the class.

The "Prequel"

Read *A Long Way From Chicago*, Richard Peck's prequel to *A Year Down Yonder*. What are the differences between the books? Use a Venn diagram to compare the similarities and differences between the two books. Which book did you enjoy more?

Group Book Report

This report is done by dividing up the book. Students work in groups to complete the book report. Each group then reports on their assigned section of the book. A variation of this method is to assign each group a different story element. Each group analyzes the book with their assigned story element. Groups may be assigned the story elements of plot, theme, style, characterization, and setting. How does this story element affect the book?

Character Descriptions

Brainstorm a list of descriptions for characters from the story. Be willing to back up descriptions with samples from the book. Write an analysis of what type of person you think each character is. What role do these characters play in the story? Who is the protagonist? Who is the antagonist? supporting characters? What lessons do you think we can learn from each character?

The Disappearing Chapter

Write a chapter that might have appeared in the book but did not. You may write this chapter for the beginning, the middle, or the end of the story.

Create-a-Game

Make up a game using the story as material for the game. This can be a board game or done in game-show format. Think up questions to be asked by the players of the game. Be sure to include the answers as well. Do a practice run on your game by playing it with a friend or family member to ensure that everything runs smoothly. Talk to your teacher about scheduling a time to play the game with students in your class.

A New Twist

Select two or three characters from the story. Write a new story using these characters. Be sure to come up with a new title. Select 10 vocabulary words from your new story. Choose one of the vocabulary activities on page nine to do with these words. Type the rough draft of your story into the computer so that you can check the spelling and the grammar.

Technology Update

Make a video recording of your favorite part of the story. Have family members or friends play the parts of characters in the story. Dress up and wear things that Mary Alice and the other characters from the story would have worn. This project will require some practice. Show your finished video to the class.

Historical-Fiction Analysis

A Year Down Yonder is an historical fiction book. The story takes place in 1937, during the Great Depression of the United States. An historical-fiction book is a fictional book that is written about a specific period in history. Though historical-fiction books are fictional, the facts and events that occur in the story relating to history must be true and accurate. There are many historical-fiction books that are not written well. A well-written book blends the story of the characters seamlessly with the events of history.

Use the following criteria to analyze *A Year Down Yonder* by Richard Peck. You may need to research information about the Great Depression to use in your analysis. (A bibliography of related books and Web sites has been provided on page 46.)

Setting

- Has the historical period in which the book takes place been accurately described? List examples of these descriptions (dress, transportation, social attitudes, etc.).
- Is the setting authentic for that time period?

Characters

- Are real historical figures mentioned in the book? List some examples.
- Are the historical figures accurately portrayed?
- Are the characters in the story portrayed realistically, as though they really lived during that time period?

Plot

- Does the plot focus on historical events and incidents? Give an example of an historical event mentioned or discussed in the book.
- Does the storyline include and incorporate historical events as they happened in history?
- Is the conflict in the book real or fictional? Could this conflict have happened during the Depression?

Details and Description

- Does Richard Peck provide accurate information about the Depression in descriptions of events in the story?

Theme

- What is the theme of this book? Does it reflect a theme from the Great Depression?
- Is there more than one theme in this book?

Historical Fiction Analysis

- What grade would you give Richard Peck on your historical fiction analysis?
- Why did you give that grade?
- Why do you think Richard Peck chose to write about this particular time in history?
- What social condition in history does this book portray?

Mary Alice or Me?

Understanding the main character can make it easier to relate to the story. Some characters are easy to relate to, while others may leave us feeling empty. We bring our life experiences to everything we read. Often, we visualize the setting and the plot based on our own personal views. What are your thoughts about Mary Alice and her story? How is her life different than yours? Select three or more of the following activities to complete. You will be sharing your work with a small group of students.

1. Write a list of 20 questions that you have for Mary Alice. You may ask things such as: How does it feel to live away from your parents? Why do you like Royce McNabb? Who would you consider to be your closest friend? Answer these questions in the way that you think Mary Alice would answer them.

2. Make a time line with small pictures documenting the year that Mary Alice spent with Grandma Dowdel. Be sure to list the events in chronological order. Add bits of information next to each event listed. Have you ever had a year that was so different than any other you had experienced? Write about this year. What were the things that happened to make it so different?

3. Mary Alice has many different challenges in her life. Make a list of challenges that she had to face while living with Grandma Dowdel. What strategies does Mary Alice use to overcome these challenges? What things have you done to meet your challenges? What have you found to be helpful when you are going through a hard time?

4. If Mary Alice could pick someone to come be a part of her story, who would it be? Would it be a family member or a new friend? Create a new character and write a description of the looks and personality of this character. Explain why Mary Alice would welcome this character. Who do you wish was in your life? Write a paragraph about this person and explain why you think it would be great to have him or her in your life.

5. Create a reader's theater script about an event from *A Year Down Yonder*. Enlist the help of other students and present the reader's theater to the class. You play the role of Mary Alice. How does she sound? What kind of expressions does she use? What is her personality like?

6. Write a letter to Mary Alice telling her what you think about Royce McNabb. Is this somebody you think she should be involved with? What advice do you have for Mary Alice? Your advice could be about Royce or it could be about other issues going on in her life. What advice would you have given her in relation to Mildred Burdick?

7. Listen to copies of songs that were popular during 1937. What do you think of these songs? How is your taste in music similar or different to that of Mary Alice? Listening to the radio seemed to bring comfort and release to Mary Alice. What do you do to relax? What role does music play in your life?

Issues of Today

Richard Peck has written numerous books for young adults. Through his writing, he attempts to address issues and problems that young adults face. Just what are these issues? Make a list of the 10 issues that you think young people deal with today. Rank them in order from most serious to least serious.

1. _____

2. _____

3. _____

4. _____

5. _____

6. _____

7. _____

8. _____

9. _____

10. _____

Now share your list with the class. Are there any duplications? Create a class list of the most commonly mentioned issues.

Questions to Consider

◆ What do you think are the solutions to these problems and issues?

◆ Select one of the issues on the class list and research the issue.

◆ How is this issue affecting young people today?

◆ What are the statistics of young people involved with these issues?

◆ How can local, state, and federal government agencies help with these issues?

◆ Was this an issue that Mary Alice or other young adults in *A Year Down Yonder* faced during the 1930s?

Critical-Thinking Activities

Now that you have completed this literature study of *A Year Down Yonder*, you are prepared to share what you have learned. Read through this list of critical thinking activities. These activities are based on Bloom's Taxonomy. Bloom's Taxonomy states that there are different levels of understanding. The levels of understanding in Bloom's Taxonomy are *knowledge* (observing and recalling information, dates, ideas, and places), *comprehension* (understanding information, interpreting facts, inferring causes), *application* (using information, methods, concepts, and theories in a new setting), *analysis* (recognizing patterns, recognizing hidden meanings), *synthesis,* (using old ideas to create new ones, predicting, drawing conclusions), and *evaluation* (comparing and discriminating between ideas, assessing and evaluating ideas and theories).

Select one project from each category of Bloom's Taxonomy. Fill out the critical thinking activities contract on page 42 and give it to your teacher.

Knowledge

❑ Make a game with index cards. On half of the cards, write statements made by characters from the story; and on the other half, write the names of people who made the statements. Share this game with other classmates. See if classmates can match the cards.

❑ Make a chart of the New Deal programs and list the impact of the New Deal on the American people.

❑ Make a crossword puzzle using the names of prominent people during the Depression.

❑ Draw a picture of someone who experienced the Depression first-hand. Write a summary of your picture on the back.

❑ Create a mind map with Grandma Dowdel's name in the center of the map. Brainstorm as many words as you can think of to use to describe Grandma Dowdel.

Comprehension

❑ Research what happened after some of the New Deal programs were passed. Write a newspaper article detailing the results of these programs.

❑ Create a time line of events that took place during the 1930s and 1940s. Did life improve after the Depression?

❑ Write and illustrate a historical-fiction story about this time period in United States history. Share your book with younger students to teach them about the subject.

❑ Create a reader's theater with parts for students to read. This should be explaining how people might have felt while going through the experience of the Depression and how they tried to put their lives back together once the Depression was over.

Application

❑ Read the "prequel" *A Long Way from Chicago* by Richard Peck. Write a new ending to the story *A Year Down Yonder*. Enlist the help of other students to act out this new ending.

❑ Pretend that you have just been elected president of the United States right after the Depression. Prepare a speech that will be heard all over the country and present it as an oral presentation to the class. This will be similar to the "Fireside Chats" for which Roosevelt was so famous.

❑ Create a poster that shows examples and give a brief summary of how some of the New Deal programs changed lives. Make the poster bright and colorful.

Critical-Thinking Activities *(cont.)*

Analysis

- ❑ Compare and contrast the difference between how things were economically during the 1930s and how they are now.

- ❑ Prepare a report on what individuals learned after experiencing the Depression. For this report, you may wish to interview individuals who lived through the Depression. Be sure to include a bibliography.

- ❑ Organize and participate in a classroom debate on solutions to problems of the economic recession of the late 1980s. You should also debate solutions to some of the problems that still exist today.

Synthesis

- ❑ Find three fictional books written during the time period of the Depression. Just look at the titles. Select one and create a story from one of those titles. Once your story is complete, read the original story and see if your story is similar. Complete the historical fiction analysis on page 37. How did you do on writing a historical fiction book?

- ❑ Imagine you are a person living through the Depression. Choose your age, the place where you lived, and your circumstances. Write a diary account of daily thoughts and activities.

- ❑ Write the lyrics and music to a song that is about life during the Depression. Perform your song before the class. You may wish to teach the song to your classmates. Your song might become a new hit!

Evaluation

- ❑ Write an editorial for the newspaper on your evaluation of the action the government took to address the concerns of the Depression. Be sure to review the actions of both presidents. Type your letter to the editor. Design a letterhead on which to type your letter.

- ❑ Interview an individual about his or her experiences of living through the Depression. After the interview, write an essay on what you have learned after doing the interview. What things will you change in your life and what have you learned?

- ❑ Compare the time of the Depression to another event in United States or world history. Write an evaluation on how individuals with power handled these situations. Give an oral report on your event. Following your report, lead a class discussion on this subject.

Optional Project

(You may select one optional project to replace one of the assigned projects above.)

Category: _____

Description of Project: _____

_____

_____

Critical-Thinking Activities Contract

Fill out the contract below and review it with your teacher. You need to select one activity to complete for each category. If you choose to create your own project, be sure to get approval before you begin. If you have any questions, ask your teacher.

Student Name _____

The activities that I have selected for each category are:

Knowledge: _____ due on _____

Comprehension: _____ due on _____

Application: _____ due on _____

Analysis: _____ due on _____

Synthesis: _____ due on _____

Evaluation: _____ due on _____

What do I need to complete these projects? _____

_____

_____

_____

_____

_____

_____

How will I share my finished projects?

_____

_____

_____

_____

_____

_____

_____   _____
Student Signature   Teacher Signature

Unit Test

Matching: Match the descriptions with the correct people. Write the correct name in the blank.

Arnold Green	Mildred Burdick	Royce McNabb
Mary Alice	Grandma Dowdel	

1. _____ is a feisty yet caring woman.

2. _____ is a talented painter.

3. _____ is excellent in math.

4. _____ is from Chicago but learns to enjoy living in the small town.

5. _____ claims Mary Alice owed her a dollar.

True or False: Write **true** or **false** next to each statement below.

1. _____ Carleen Lovejoy was furious when she thought that Ina-Rae got a Valentine from Royce McNabb.

2. _____ Royce McNabb was the author of "Newsy Notes."

3. _____ Bootsie had a kitten named April.

4. _____ Mary Alice managed to get the part of Mary in the Christmas program.

5. _____ The cherry tarts Grandma made for the DAR were burned and ruined.

Short Answer: Answer each question with a complete sentence.

1. How does Mary Alice feel at the beginning of the story about going to live with Grandma?

_____

2. Why do you think Grandma kept Bootsie the cat? _____

_____

3. How was Grandma able to help Mrs. Abernathy and her son?_____

_____

4. What is the relationship between Grandma and Old Man Nyquist like? _____

_____

5. How does Grandma show that she loves Mary Alice? _____

_____

Essays: On the back of this paper, write short-essay answers to these questions.

1. Do you think Grandma is a good or bad person? Be sure to support your answer with examples.

2. How did living with her Grandma impact Mary Alice's life in a positive way?

Reflections

Teacher note: Choose the appropriate number of quotations to which your students should respond.

1. Mother gave me a quick squeeze before she let me go.   And I could swear I heard her murmur, "Better you than me."

2. "Hoo-boy," Grandma said. "Another mouth to feed." Her lips pleated. "And what's that thing?" she nodded to my other hand.

3. Grandma nodded. "Boys is bad businesses," she said, quite agreeable for her. "Though girls is worse."

4. I teetered on the threshold. When Grandma loomed up behind me, all three boys in the classroom threw up their hands and hollered out, "Don't shoot! We give up!"

5. "Don't cross her. Better settle with her," Ina-Rae whispered in return. "She'll foller you home. She does that."

6. With a tire hung on its radiator. "Grandma, that wasn't stealing was it? I mean, in your opinion."

7. Grandma looked at that dime like she'd never seen one. Her eyes were circles of astonishment. "That won't do it, L.J.," she said, loud. Mr. Weidenbach winced. The porch sagged with customers of his bank.

8. "Grandma, why were you out tramping the countryside in this weather?" "First snow," she explained. "It's my busy season. It's all work, work, work. I'll die standing up like an old ox."

9. Grandma said, louder than before, "If you can, get the bootlace loose from around your wallet. The boys who fought at the front didn't count the cost."

10. "It looks like riches to me," Mrs. Abernathy murmured. "And it'll have to see us through."

11. "What would your paw think if I kept you?" she said finally. "I don't want your maw after me." "Grandma, Mother's terrified of you. She always was. You know that."

12. "I'm a stranger here myself," Royce said. "I'm from Mattoon. You're from Chicago. We're a couple of foreigners here."

13. "Why not? It's a better climate than New York," said Grandma, who'd never been there. "It's the healthiest spot in Illinois. We had to hang a man to start the graveyard."

Conversations

Directions: Work in size-appropriate groups to write and perform the conversations that might have occurred in each of the following situations:

- Before leaving the train station, Mary Alice talks with her mother about leaving and the things to expect while living at Grandma's. (*2 persons*)

- After the first week of living with Grandma, Mary Alice talks on the telephone to her mother about her experiences. (*2 persons*)

- Mary Alice runs into Mildred Burdick in town, and they talk about what happened with Grandma after the first day of school. (*2 persons*)

- The townspeople discuss how bossy Grandma was when she collected money for the burgoo. (*3–4 persons*)

- Reba Pensinger confronts Grandma about stealing pumpkins from her yard. (*2 persons*)

- Augie Fluke and Mr. Fluke talk as they try to get the glue off of Augie's head. (*2 persons*)

- The Legionnaire speaks with Augie Fluke about his Buick. (*2 persons*)

- Joey and Mary Alice talk the night he comes to visit her for the Christmas program. (*2 persons*)

- Carleen finds out that Mary Alice wrote the valentines to Ina-Rae. She gives an earful to Mary Alice. Mary Alice responds with a mind of her own. (*2 persons*)

- The women at the next DAR meeting discuss the disaster that took place at the DAR meeting at Grandma's house. (*5 persons*)

- Arnold Green speaks with Maxine Patch after the incident at Grandma's. (*2 persons*)

- Royce McNabb speaks with Mary Alice the next time he sees her after the Maxine Patch incident. (*2 persons*)

- A group of townspeople share their feelings of what they think about Grandma. (*4 persons*)

- Before Mary Alice leaves for Chicago, she and Grandma share memories and reminisce about their year together. (*2 persons*)

Bibliography of Related Sources

Fiction

Cochrane, Patricia A. *Purely Rosie Pearl*. Bantam Books, 1997.

De Young, C. Coco. *A Letter to Mrs. Roosevelt*. Delacorte Press, 1999.

Defelice, Cynthia C. *Nowhere to Call Home*. Farrar Straus & Giroux, 1999.

Ducey, Jean Sparks. *The Bittersweet Time*. Wm. B. Eeedrmans Publishing Co., 1995.

Hamilton, Virginia. *Drylongso*. Harcourt Brace, 1997.

Hesse, Karen. *Out of the Dust*. Scholastic Trade, 1997.

Koller, Jackie French. *Nothing to Fear*. Harcourt Brace, 1993.

Myers, Anna. *Red-Dirt Jessie*. Puffin, 1997.

Porter, Tracy. *Treasures in the Dust*. HarperCollins, 1997.

Raven, Margot. *Angels in the Dust*. Bridgewater, 1997.

Recorvits, Helen. *Goodbye Walter Malinski*. Frances Foster Books, 1999.

Taylor, Mildred. *Song of the Trees*. Laureleaf, 1996.

Thesman, Jean. *The Storyteller's Daughter*. Houghton Mifflin, 1997.

Willis, Patricia. *The Barn Burner*. Houghton Mifflin, 2000.

Nonfiction

Freedman, Russell. *Franklin Delano Roosevelt*. Clarion Books, 1992.

Galbraith, John Kenneth. *The Great Crash: 1929*. Houghton Mifflin, 1997.

Kartchner Clark, Sarah. *The Great Depression*. (Thematic Unit). Teacher Created Resources, 1999.

Shebar, Sharon, & Lippincott, Gary. *Franklin D. Roosevelt & the New Deal*. Barrons Juveniles, 1987.

Watkins, T.H. *The Great Depression*. Little, Brown & Co., 1993.

Videos

FDR: The Man Who Changed America. (1 hour) Phoenix Films, New York, NY. (212) 684-5910.

Franklin Delano Roosevelt. CRM/McGraw-Hill Films, Del Mar, CA 92014. (714) 453-5000.

The Great Depression. PBS Video, Alexandria, Virginia. (703) 739-5000.

Journey of Natty Gann. Walt Disney Home Video, 1985.

The Roosevelt Years Series. Films Incorporated, Wilmette, Illinois. (312) 256-6600.

Web Sites

The Web sites listed below have been reviewed and selected for use on the topic of the Great Depression. To access these sites, type in the URLs listed. (Because Internet sites are constantly changing, you may prefer to use keywords like "Great Depression" on a Web browser.)

The American Memory Library of Congress—*http://memory.loc.gov*

American Memory Library of Congress offers lesson plans for teachers of American History.

National Archives and Records Administration—*http://www.nara.gov/exhall/newdeal/newdeal.html*

A Web site sponsored by the National Archives offering Depression-era artwork, interviews, and more.

The New Deal Network—*http://newdeal.feri.org*
Web site featuring photographs, political cartoons, original speeches and memos, and lesson plans for teachers about the Great Depression. There are over 3,000 items found at this site.

Answer Key

Page 10

1. Accept appropriate summaries.
2. Mary Alice is 15 years old.
3. Mom, Dad, her brother Joey, and Mary Alice
4. Her dad lost his job and her parents didn't have enough room in their rental.
5. The story takes place in a small town outside of Chicago in the year 1937.
6. Grandma Dowdel is a big, tall woman that seems to show little affection.
7. She bought her cat, Bootsie, and a radio. Grandma took her to high school.
8. The grades are combined into mixed classes and the school seems run down.
9. Mildred says Mary Alice lied, but mostly it's Mildred's way of getting a buck. Grandma distracts Mildred and sends her walking home.
10. Ina-Rae is friendly. Mary Alice is a city girl from Chicago.

Page 15

1. Accept appropriate summaries.
2. Pecan and pumpkin pies
3. Gooseberry pie would not be made with fresh ingredients.
4. They knocked the pecans out of Old Man Nyquist's tree with his tractor, and they "stole" the pumpkins.
5. She'll replace the pumpkins with a pumpkin pie.
6. She used her own recipe of thick and sticky glue. The pranksters tripped over the wire and Grandma poured the glue on their heads.
7. His head had been shaved and his scalp was rubbed raw and beginning to scab. His nose was bandaged.
8. There seems to be mixed feelings, but most are afraid of her. She is not someone with whom to mess!
9. They loved the pies and showered Grandma with compliments.
10. A rusted-out tin can was tied to her tail with twine.

Page 18

A.
2. I | will respond
3. She | skis
4. Andy | swims

B.
6. dog | jumped — A, big, happily
7. baby | clapped — The, funny, joyfully
8. men | yelled — Two, angry, loudly
9. teacher | spoke — The, new, well

Page 20

1. Accept appropriate summaries.
2. The cold was nothing compared to when Grandma was little.
3. A turkey shoot is an outing where the men use air rifles to shoot paper cut-outs.
4. She stated that she wouldn't qualify and showed no interest in joining.
5. She pressured the people she thought could afford it to pay more per cup of the burgoo.
6. He accidentally shot the tire of a man's black Buick.
7. He was shot and gassed in the trenches during WWI.
8. She went to check her fox traps.
9. Instead of the doll that was supposed to be there, there was a real baby in the manger the night of the performance. The attention went to the baby instead of Carleen. The baby was Mildred Burdick's.
10. Mary Alice's brother Joey was the guest. Grandma sold the fox money to buy the ticket.

Answer Key (cont.)

Page 25

1. Accept appropriate summaries.

2. Mary Alice is writing the "Newsy Notes."

3. DAR is Daughters of the American Revolution. Grandma was asked to bring cherry tarts.

4. Royce is a new student. He comes from Matoon. She thinks he is cute and likes him.

5. Mary Alice secretly sends them as though she were Royce McNabb and some other secret admirers. Carleen is furious and throws a fit.

6. That Wilhelmina Roach is really the sister of Mrs. Effie Wilcox.

7. Bourbon was added to the punch.

8. (Answers may vary.) to humble the ladies that were members of the DAR

9. souvenir of Starved Rock, Illinois

10. Answers will vary.

Page 28

1.–3. Answers will vary.

4. $10 a week.

5.–6. Answers may vary.

Page 30

1. Accept appropriate summaries.

2. Bootsie brought many things and put them on Mary Alice's bed, but the best surprise was a little kitten that Mary Alice named April.

3. She invited Royce McNabb to tutor her.

4. That they are both from out of town.

5. Maxine Patch was posing nude for Arnold Green's painting when a snake in Grandma's attic fell down on her. She screamed and went running out. Grandma alerted the town to Maxine as she ran home.

6. She shot the bullets from the Winchester into the air.

7. They all "woke up" and went to see what was happening. They saw Maxine Patch running through the town without any clothes on.

8. She wanted to hook up Arnold Green and Miss Butler, though she claimed it was to improve Mary Alice's grades.

9. She wanted to make sure her Grandma was alright. Old Man Nyquist was the first person Grandma checked on.

10. They have learned to love and appreciate each other. They care about each other a great deal. Mary Alice comes back to Royce McNabb in Grandma's home. (Answers will vary.)

Page 43

Matching

1. Grandma Dowdel

2. Arnold Green

3. Royce McNabb

4. Mary Alice

5. Mildred Burdick

True or False

1. True

2. False

3. True

4. True

5. False

Short Answer

1. She is not very happy. She is afraid of Grandma and doesn't want to go by herself without her brother.

2. So that Mary Alice would want to come back and because she had gotten used to it

3. By raising as much money as she could at the turkey shoot for the Abernathy's

4. They yell and argue, but deep down they are friends and care about each other.

5. Though she seems gruff and grouchy, she cares for and loves Mary Alice. She does many things like raising money to buy tickets for Christmas.

Essay

Answers will vary.